Dickens Dramatized Seri

OLIVER TW

The 1838 Theatrical Adaptation

By George Almar

Adapted from the Novel by Charles Dickens

TAP

Theatre Arts Press

Classic and Noteworthy Plays

Published from primary sources and other historical records.

For a complete list of titles visit

TheatreArtsPress.com

Printed in the United States of America

9 8 7 6 5 4 3 2 1

"The stage is never devoted to a more noble or better purpose than when it lends its powerful aid to improve the morals and correct the vices of the ages. It is this conviction which has led to the adaptation of the impressive work upon which this drama is founded, opening one of the darkest volumes of life, and revealing facts that must startle the more strongly, from the previous total ignorance of their existence, even by those persons residing in the very heart of the scenes in which they are daily and nightly passing.

Thus it will be seen in this Drama. Its great original, who, very badly speaking, may truly be termed akin to Hogarth, has raised a beacon on the basis of truth to warn the erring, guide the inexperience, instruct the ignorant to avoid the shoals by which they are surrounded, and forcibly inculcate the great moral lesson that vice, however prosperous for a time, will sooner or later meet with punishment and disgrace, while virtue, whatever be its trials and temptations will ultimately secure a lasting and just reward."

Management, Surrey Theatre, 1838

OLIVER TWIST was first performed on November 19, 1838 at the Surrey Theatre, London with the following cast:

Oliver Twist........................ Master Owne
Mr. Brownlow................................ Mr. Cooper
Mr. Grimwig.................................. Mr. Cullen
Monks.. Mr. Simpson
Bumble.. Mr. W. Smith
Noah.. Master Young
Bill Skies.. Mr. E. F. Saville
Toby Crackitt................................. Mr. G. Almar
Fagin.. Mr. Heslop
The Dodger.................................... Mr. Ross
Charley Bates................................. Mr. France
Rose Maylie.................................... Miss Collett
Miss Nancy.................................... Miss Martin
Mrs. Corney................................... Mrs. W. Daly
Mrs. Bedwin................................... Mrs. Lewis

ACT I

SCENE I

The house of Mrs. Cornet, an interior, fireplace on one side, with a glass over the mantel-piece, according to the etching of the history, and Mrs. Cornet discovered sitting beside the fire; a small round table in front of it, on which the tea equipage is placed.

MRS. CORNET. *(Shuddering.)* What a bleak, dark, and frightful night! Now then to solace myself with a cup of tea. *(Pours hot water from kettle on the hob into the teapot.)* Well, I'm sure we have all on us a great deal to be grateful for— a great deal, if we did but know it. *(In the pouring the tea, the water overflows and scalds her fingers)* Drat the pot! a little stupid thing, that only holds a couple of cups! What use is it of to anybody—except, except to a poor desolate creature like me, oh dear! This small teapot and the single cup awakes in my mind the recollections of my poor dead and gone Mr. Corney. Ah I—I shall never get another like him. *(Sips her tea, when a soft tap is heard at the door without.)* There! disturbed again! Who would be matron to the workhouse of Mudfog! *(Knock somewhat louder.)* Oh! come in with you! some of the old women dying, I suppose; drat 'em! They always die when I'm at meals — don't stand there letting the cold air in, don't ! What's amiss now, eh!

(Voice without.)

BUMBLE. Nothing, ma'am, nothing.

MRS. CORNET. Dear me. *(In a tone pianissimo.)* Is that Mr. Bumble?

BUMBLE. At your service, ma'am.

(Enter Mr. Bumble, through the door, He shakes the snow which has accumulated on his coat from it, bearing his cocked hat in one hand and his bundle in the other, with hesitation.)

BUMBLE. Shall I shut the door, ma'am?

MRS. CORNET. Why, Mr. Bumble! to be open with you—

BUMBLE. Exactly so, ma'am — I'll shut it.

(Closes the door and slowly comes forward.)

MRS. CORNET. Hard weather, Mr. Bumble!

BUMBLE. Hardy indeed! Anti-parochial weather, ma'am. We have given away, Mrs. Corney, a manner of twenty quarter loaves and a cheese and a half this blessed afternoon—and yet them paupers are not contented.

MRS. CORNET. Of course not. When would they be, Mr. Bumble?

BUMBLE. When, indeed, ma'am! The great principle of our poor relief is to give the paupers exactly what they don't want, and then they'll get tired of coming.

MRS. CORNET. Dear me! Well, that is a good one, too.

BUMBLE. So you see, ma'am, that if a sick family wants candles, give 'em gruel; and if they want gruel, give 'em cheese. *(Taking two bottles from his pocket and placing them on table.)* This is the port wine, ma'am, that the Board ordered for the Infirmary — real, fresh, genuine port wine, only out of the cask this afternoon; clear as a bell, and not no sediment. Good evening ma'am. *(Takes up hat to go.)*

MRS. CORNET. You'll have a very cold walk, Mr. Bumble.

BUMBLE. It blows, ma'am—*(turning up collar)*—enough to cut one's ears off.

MRS. CORNET. Mr. Bumble — sir!

BUMBLE. Mrs. Corney — ma'am!

MRS. CORNET. Perhaps you'll just sit down and take a cup of tea, Mr. Bumble.

(BUMBLE instantaneously turns back his collar, places his hat and stick upon a chair, and draws another chair up to the table; as he slowly seats himself he looks at the lady; she fixes her eyes upon the little teapot; BUMBLE smiles and coughs slightly, MRS. CORNET rises to get another cup and saucer from the closet as she sits down, her eyes again encounter those of the Beadle.)

MRS. CORNET. How, how you look at me, Mr. Bumble!

BUMBLE. Can't help it, ma'am.

MRS. CORNET. Sweet, Mr. Bumble! *(Sweetening tea.)*

BUMBLE. Very sweety Mrs. Corney. *(She hands over the tea, BUMBLE spreads a handkerchief over his knees, to prevent the crumbs sullying them; begins to eat and drink, occasionally heaving deep sighs,)* I perceive you keep a cat ma'am.

MRS. CORNET. I do — I am so fond of them.

BUMBLE. A nice animal, and so very domestic.

MRS. CORNET. Very; and so fond of their home.

BUMBLE. Mrs. Corney, ma'am. *(Waving his teaspoon, and slowly marking the time with it as he speaks.)* I mean to say this: that any cat or kitten that could live with you, ma'am, and not be fond of its home, must be a ass.

MRS. CORNET. Oh! Mr. Bumble!

BUMBLE. It's no use disguising facts. *(Flourishing hi spoon.)* I would drown it myself with pleasure.

MRS. CORNET. You are a cruel man — and a very 'ard 'arted man, Mr. Bumble.

BUMBLE. 'Ard 'arted, ma'am? *(During this conversation BUMBLE has gradually lessened the distance between himself and MRS. CORNEY — the final hitch he gives to his chair brings it contiguous to that of the lady.)* 'Ard 'rted! Are you 'ard 'arted yourself, Mrs. Gomey?

MRS. CORNET. What a very curious question for a single man!What can you want so know for, Mr. Bumble?*(BUMBLE empties his cup, finishes a piece of toast, whisks the crumbs off his knees, wipes his lips, and deliberately kisses the matron.)* Mr. Bumble. *(In a whisper.)* Mr. Bumble, I shall scream.

(BUMBLE makes no reply, but in a slow and dignified manner, puts his arm round the matron's waist, while a hasty knock at the door is heard; BUMBLE darts up with much agility to the wine bottles and begins dusting them with great violence ; then pets the cat; MRS. CORNEY rises as rapidly.)

MRS. CORNET. Who, who's there?

(SUSAN putting her head through the half-opened door.)

SUSAN. If you please, old Sally is going fast, ma'am.

MRS. CORNET. Well! what's that to me? I can't keep her alive, can I?

SUSAN. No—no, mistress! Nobody can. But she's troubled in her mind; and she says she's got something to tell you, which you must hear, and — and she'll never die quiet till you come, mistress. *(Exits.)*

MRS. CORNET. Don't go away till I come back again, Mr. Bumble; I shan't be more than a minute or two at the most, Mr. Bumble.

BUMBLE. And while you are gone every minute will seem to me a month, Mrs. Corney.

MRS. CORNET. Heigho! Mr. Bumble.

BUMBLE. Heigho! Mrs. Corney. *(Exit MRS. CORNET.)* The business of the board must not be neglected. Here's my porochial book. Let me see — porochial apprentices — Abraham — Benjamin. Yes, here they are alphabetically deranged! Nathaniel — Obadiah — Oliver — Oliver Twist. Ah! that's the last orphan the parish, thanks to Mr. Sowerberry, the undertaker, has thrown off its shoulders. He's 'prenticed at last, that's some comfort. But of all the artful and designing orphans that ever I did see, he's one of the most barefacedest! Well! he'll come to be hung, that's sure! Memorandum. Ah! I thought I had made one. This Oliver was the child of a poor pale-faced, ladyfied-looking girl who came one night to the workhouse, where she died. I wonder who she was.

(Enter MRS. CORNET.)

MRS. CORNET. Well, she is dead.

BUMBLE. *(Starting.)* Who is dead?

MRS. CORNET. Old Sally; but I'll tell you all about it, Mr. Bumble.

BUMBLE. Do, Mrs. Corney — pray do!

MRS. CORNET. Fifteen years ago this very winter, there comes a knock, and a low moan at that very door. I opened it with fear and trembling — for it was a past 12 o'clock, and it snowed and blowed, as I never seed it afore; there was a poor young creature with a child in her arms, looking up with such a pitiful face, and a begging for shelter in the workhouse, so of course we taken her in; she didn't trouble us long, though, for she seemed to fade away from the moment she entered the workhouse. And the night she died, Old Sally was a nursing her, she asked to see her little boy to bless him before she took her long journey; I brought the little creature from his crib. She put her thin, wasted hand, on his little golden head, and the little fellow seemed to smile in her face; "Oh my God," said she, "protect thy lonely and desolate child, abandoned to the mercies of mankind," and so she died. *(Seeing BUMBLE sniveling.)* The dear, good man, why, he's quite overcome with grief at the story.

BUMBLE. As who would not be.

MRS. CORNET. The boy was called Oliver Twist.

BUMBLE. Oliver Twist, the one we've just 'prenticed to the undertaker?

MRS. CORNET. The same.

BUMBLE. But what's this to do with Old Sally, that's just dead?

MRS. CORNET. Why, as I told you. Old Sally nursed her that night, and when she was dead, robbed the body of this locket and ring. See how curious they are, and here, cut on the inside, is the name of the poor lady, I suppose, A. G. N. E. S.

BUMBLE. Agnes! and that's all?

MRS. CORNET. What a pity they didn't put the rest of the name there.

BUMBLE. Mrs. Cornet, you are not only a genus, but a wenus. Oh, when shall we become one flesh. Mrs. Cornet, oh, picture to yourself, myself standing at the Haltar before the priest. The charity boys a singing, oh! Mrs. Cornet. *(Exeunt.)*

SCENE II

Kitchen at Mr. Sowerberry's.

OLIVER discovered.

OLIVER. This is a strange place, and I feel so chill and desolate here; poor little Dick. I shall never see him again. I have no friends to care for, and none to care for me now. When I crept into my narrow bed last night, my heart was so heavy that I wished it had been my coffin, and that I could be laid in a calm and lasting sleep in the churchyard, with the tall grass waving gently above my head. And the sound of the old deep bell to sooth me in my slumber. *(Knock at door.)* Who's there?

NOAH. *(Outside.)* Open the door, can't ye?

OLIVER. *(Opens door.)* I will, sir.

(Enter Noah.)

NOAH. You're a nice one, do you want to freeze me?

OLIVER. No sir, please.

NOAH. You're the new boy, ain't you

OLIVER. Yes sir.

NOAH. And a very new boy you look. You're the one they got from the verkus, eh?

OLIVER. Yes sir.

NOAH. You're too small for the business.

OLIVER. But I'll grow, I hope, won't I

NOAH. I'm glad he's a little un, cause I can wallop him when I wants to keep my hand in. How old are you, verkus?

OLIVER. Fourteen; I beg pardon, sir, but do you want a coffin?

NOAH. I tell you what, you'll want a coffin if you cuts your jokes on your superiors; don't you know who I am?

OLIVER. No, sir.

NOAH. Well, then, I'm Mister Noah Claypole, head boy here, and your superior, does you hear, verkus?

(Enter CHARLOTTE, with supper.)

CHARLOTTE. Here, you boys, bold your noise; what's the matter with you?

NOAH. Matter enough. The new boy's been insulting me.

OLIVER. Indeed, I didn't mean —

CHARLOTTE. There, there, that will do. Come to supper.

(They go to table and sit.)

OLIVER. I'm not hungry.

NOAH. Well, then, I am. *(Eats voraciously.)* And so you ain't hungry?

OLIVER. No. Noah, I am not hungry. Noah

OLIVER. My heart is too full to talk,.

NOAH. Yes, and so is my mouth. Here's a 'ead o' 'air for a cat to kitten in. My wig, how it curls, verkus. *(Teasing OLIVER.)*

OLIVER. Yours don't, Noah.

NOAH . No, mine's just like myself, right up and down, and straight-forward. You ought to know that I'm your superior, because I told you so, verkus. "Fair change is no robbery," so you shall eat my fat, and I'll eat your lean, verk'us,

OLIVER. You may take it all, and welcome!

NOAH. I will, verk'us.

CHARLOTTE. Lor, Noah! Why don't you let the boy alone?

NOAH. Let him alone! Why everybody lets him alone for the matter of that. His father and mother will never interfere with him, nor his relations, neither.

CHARLOTTE. Oh you queer soul, an't you funny?

NOAH. He is such a sneak; an't he, Charlotte

OLIVER. What is a sneak, Noah Claypole!

NOAH. By goms, if this isn't blessed ignorance. Do you mean for to come, for to go, for to say you don't know what's a sneak?

OLIVER. No! Is it anything like you, Noah?

NOAH. Oh, carry me out and bury me, if this an't pretty imperence — I say, verk'us, how's yer mother?

OLIVER. She's dead! Don't you say anything about her to me!

NOAH. What did she die of, verk'us?

OLIVER. Of a broken heart; if the nurse told me true. I think, I almost know, what it must be to die of that.

(OLIVER seems affected.)

NOAH. Tol de rol, lol lol, right fol lairy. What's set you a snivelling now?

OLIVER. Not you.

NOAH. Oh, not me, right!

OLIVER. There — that's enough! Don't say anything to me about her, you'd better not.

Noah. Well, better not! Don't be impendent. Your mother, too! She was a nice un! Oh, Lor! yer know it can't be helped now, and of course yer couldn't help it then, and I'm very sorry for it; we all are, and pity yer very much. But yer must know, yer mother was a regular, right down bad un!

OLIVER. What did you say?

NOAH. A regular, right down bad un; and it's a great deal better, verk'us, that she died when she did, or she'd ha' been transported or hung.

(OLIVER furiously springs up, overturns the table and chairs, seizes NOAH by the throat, shakes him in the violence of his rage, then collects his whole force into one heavy blow, and fells him to the ground. NOAH falls.)

SCENE III

Road near Barnet.

Enter DODGER.

DODGER. My heyes and precious limbs, how tired my beautiful legs are, and nothing for my trouble, neither; ha! ha! what a go that was last night: I opened a gentleman's window for the purpose of examining his spoons, and when I got inside I was so frightened I couldn't get out again, and this morning, by way of cooling my ardor, they put me under the pump, refreshed me with its cool and pleasant water. Won't Charley Bates and Old Fagin shout and bust their buttons off when I tells 'em,

(Enter Oliver.)

OLIVER. I have escaped them; I listened to their taunts without an ansry word, I bore the lash without a cry; but when they spoke wild thoughts about my mother — Well! well! I mustn't think. Oh, cold, stiff, and hungry, I could lay down and die.

(Leans against a tree — DODGER advances.)

DODGER. Hollo! my covey. What's the row?

OLIVER. The row! I don't hear any; do you, sir?

DODGER. I mean what are you at, what are you arter?

OLIVER. I am very hungry and tired.

DODGER. I'm low water mark myself; but so far as it goes, I'll fork out; so up with your pins, and I'll see what's for breakfast. *(Takes bread, meat and bottle from his pocket.)* First, there's a fourpenny bran; next, there's sixpenny worth of ham; and here, a toothful of port. There, eat, drink, and make your life happy.

OLIVER. You are a strange boy, but no doubt a good one.

DODGER. Good as gold, and as brazy about the frontispiece as a bed-warmer. You might trust me with your pus, and no mistake—*(aside)*—when there's nothing in it. To come to the pint, name's Dawkins, John Dawkins; by some I'm called the Dodger, and by some I'm called the Artful Dodger. Where I lives you shall live too, if you like; and how I lives is just the best way I can. Going to London?

OLIVER. Yes.

DODGER. Got any lodgings?

OLIVER. No.

DODGER. Money?

OLIVER. No.

(The DODGER whistles.)

DODGER. I suppose you want some place to sleep to-night, don't you?

OLIVER. I do, indeed.

DODGER. There, don't fret your eyelids; come along; I know a 'spectable gentleman as lives in London, wot'll give you lodgings for no-think, and never ask for change; and don't he know me — oh, not in — not in the least— by no means — certainly not.

OLIVER. But if he doesn't know you, you are a stranger.

DODGER. Oil, yes, over the bender; so tip your rags a gallop, and flare up at both ends, my covey.

(Exeunt OLIVER and DODGER.)

Scene IV

Fagin's den, a mister able garret. — a fire, over which FAGIN is discovered cooking; nearby, a clotheshorse, on which handkerchiefs are hanging. — a table, round which are seated several boys, smoking and drinking. — Loud laughing.

FAGIN. Hush—there is somebody on the stairs— quiet — quiet. *(He goes to the door, and calls through the keyhole.)* Who's there? *(A whistle is heard.)* The word? *(Voice without— "Plummy and Slam.")* You may come in. (FAGIN half opens the door. But there's two of ye — who's t'other one? (Enter the DODGER and OLIVER.) Where did he come from? *(Pointing to OLIVER.)*

DODGER. From Greenland. Fagin, tip us your listener.

(FAGIN inclines his ear to DODGER, who listens.)

FAGIN. You don't say so!

DODGER. I do, though. This is my friend Oliver Twist, and this is my friend, Fagin.

FAGIN. We are glad to see you, Oliver, all of us; ain't we my teres

Omnes. Yes, yes, all of us.

(Some bonnet him, and perform sundry tricks. which the Jew puts an end to by producing a whip and cracking it loudly. They continue to tease OLIVER.)

DODGER. Leave him alone, will ye? You won't — then up, Charley, and clear the crib.

(CHARLEY BATES and the DODGER drive them off — a pause.)

FAGIN. What are you looking at, Oliver?

OLIVER. At all those handkerchiefs.

FAGIN. There are a good many of 'em, ain't there? We've just took'd 'em out ready for the wash. Ha! ha! ugh — ugh!

OLIVER You've a bad cough, sir.

FAGIN. Very, my tere, very. Will you take anything after your walk, Oliver?

OLIVER. I feel weary and should like to sleep, sir.

FAGIN. Here's a nightcap for you. *(Fills a glass of water with gin.)* Drink, Oliver, drink.

OLIVER. What's all this? *(Taking the glass from FAGIN.)*

FAGIN. Up — up! twill do you good, my tere. *(OLIVER slowly drains it, then falls into a deep slumber. FAGIN lifts him gently upon the sacks, then, on tiptoe, takes light from the table, and passes over the closed eyes of Oliver.)* He's sound for a time, and I can now, when all are at rest, steal a look at my treasures. *(FAGIN raises a trap from the floor, takes up a small box, which he places carefully on the table — he takes from it a magnificent gold watch, sparkling with diamonds.)* Aha! — clever dogs — clever dogs— and staunch to the last — never told the old parson where they were— never peached upon old Fagin — no, no; and if they had I wouldn't ha' loosened the knot. Fine fellows! fine fellows! *(FAGIN examines other trinkets.)* There's an inscription upon this, but my eyes cannot make it out from age — old age. Five of 'em were strung up together on the tree! Where shall I go when I die? No matter. *(His glance suddenly encounters that of OLIVER, who has appeared restless in his sleep. — FAGIN closer the box with a loud crash, and, laying his hand on a bread knife which was on the table, starts furiously up.)* What's that? Why do you watch me? Why are you awake? Speak out, boy, quick — for your life!

OLIVER. I wasn't able to sleep any longer. I'm very sorry if I've disturbed you.

FAGIN. You were not awake a little while ago?

OILVER. No, no, indeed, sir.

FAGIN. Are you sure?

OLIVER. I was not, indeed, sir.

FAGIN. Tush! tush! my tere, of course I only tried to frighten you. Did you see any of these pretty things, Oliver?

OLIVER. Yes, sir.

FAGIN. Ah! they're mine — all my little property — set up, set up, there's a basin just over there — and you can wash, my tere.

(OLIVER exits. FAGIN rapidly replaces the jewelry. Enter CHARLEY BATES and DODGER — OLIVER returns at the same time.)

FAGIN. Well, I hope you've been at work yesterday, my teres.

DODGER. Hard as nails.

FAGIN. Good boys! good boys! And what have you got, Charley?

CHARLEY. A couple of note-holders. *(Gives pocket-books to FAGIN.)*

FAGIN. Very neat and nicely made; Charley's a nice workman, ain't he, Oliver?

OLIVER. I never saw him at work, sir.

FAGIN. But you shall, ma tere — all in good time — you shall; and what ha' you got, Dodger?

DODGER. Wipes. *(Gives handkerchiefs to FAGIN.)*

FAGIN. That not so good, my tere; but they're in dory.

OLIVER. What are you going to do with all those handkerchiefs?

DODGER. Sew 'em together to make summer trowsers.

OLIVER. Lor! Really?

CHARLEY. Oh! button me up! Ha! ha! how green he is.

FAGIN. Now, boys, shall we have a game?

BOYS. To be sure.

FAGIN. Only to amuse Oliver; shall we, Oliver?

OLIVER. Yes, if you please, sir.

FAGIN. *(Putting on coat and hat.)* Now then, boys; I'm a banker, a nice banker, going to the city, with plenty of money, too; but I must take care of the thieves — eh, Oliver!

OLIVER. Yes, sir.

FAGIN. Here we go — here we go. *(Walks up and down. BATES steals pocket-book, and DODGER handkerchief.)* I'm robbed! stop thief! stop thief! *(BATES and DODGER hold up the- stolen property. All laugh.)* Clever dogs; clever dogs— ain't they, Oliver?

OILVER. Ha! ha! very, sir.

FAGIN. Would you like to try, Oliver?

OLIVER. Yes, if you please, sir.

FAGIN. There we go again. *(OLIVER tries and gets caught.)* Ah! I've got you. You must take it slow, slow and artistically. *(Oliver tries again and succeeds.)* A good boy, a good boy. Oliver you'll be a great man, you'll live in English history; you'll stand recorded in *(aside)* the Newgate Calendar.

DODGER. Now then, we must pad the hoof, Charley. Say good luck to us, Fagin.

FAGIN. Good fortune, ma teres. *(To DODGER.)* Take Oliver on the prowl, and try him. Yon are down on what I mean.

DODGER. Down as a hammer.

FAGIN. Good bye, Oliver; you are to go with those nice young gentlemen.

OLIVER. Thankee, sir.

FAGIN. And mind you do exactly what the nice young gentlemen tell you.

OLIVER. I will, sir.

DODGER. You hear what Fagin says, you're to do exactly what we two nice young gentlemen tells you.

OLIVER. I know I am.

DODGER. Well then, mizzle.

OLIVER I don't know how to mizzle.

DODGER. Cut your stick.

OLIVER. I haven't got a knife.

CHARLEY. My eyes! how jolly green he is.

(Exeunt.)

Scene V

A street in Clerkenwell. — A Bookseller's shop and stand.

Enter Mr. Brownlow.

BROWNLOW. 'Tis a book on ornamental gardening which I've seen somewhere here. Plague on my memory, I can't recollect the title! I'll try another book-stall! I'll give it my attention, and here I may be more successful.

(Goes to stall, and while he is anxiously employed in examining its contents, enter rapidly the DODGER, CHARLEY BATES, and OLIVER. The DODGER suddenly stops, puts his finger to his lips, then draws his companions back again with the greatest caution and circumspection.)

OLIVER. What's the matter?

DODGER. Hush! Do you see that old cove at the book-stall?

OLIVER. The old gentleman over the way? — yes, I see him.

CHARLEY. He's a prime plant.

DODGER. Yes, he'll do, Charley.

OLIVER. Do! do! What will he do for? *(They get stealthily towards the old gentleman. — The Dodger plunges his hand into the old gentleman' s pocket, draws from it a handkerchief, which he hands over to Bates, when they both run away.)* Oh, dreadful! Into what hands have I fallen! I see it now — the handkerchiefs — the jewels — the Jew.

(As he turns to move away, MR. BROWNLOW, missing his handkerchief, turns suddenly round, and exclaims, seeing OLIVER run,

BROWNLOW. Stop thief!

(Enter a BAKER and BUTCHER.)

BAKER. What's the matter?

BROWNLOW. I have been robber, sir, that's the matter. There! there he goes! Stop thief!

(Exit Mr. Brownlow, followed by others, vehemently calling "Stop thief! Stop thief!" Loud cries of "Stop thief!" without. DODGER, BATES, and OLIVER, at the top of their speed, run across a POLICEMAN, then a mass of TRADESMEN, BOYS, MARKET-WOMEN, etc. A Fat Person falls; others fall over him, delaying the pursuit. The stage eventually is cleared. Then, exhausted and almost out of breath, MR. BROWNLOW enters. He faintly calls "Stop thief!" fanning himself with his handkerchief.)

BROWNLOW A young rascal! *(Crowd utter a "Hurrah!" without.)* Ah! I see they have got him.

(They drag OLIVER., bleeding at the mouth.)

BAKER. Stand aside — give him a little air.

BUTCHER. He don't deserve it. Where's the gentleman? Oh; here he is! Make room there for the gentleman. Is this the boy, sir?

BROWNLOW Yes, that's the boy. That is — I — I am afraid it is.

BUTCHER. Afraid it is! Come, that's a good un.

BROWNLOW Poor fellow! He has hurt himself.

A TALL FELLOW *(in the crowd exclaims.)* I did that, sir; and preciously I cut my knuckles agin his mouth. I guv him the blow, sir. Preluips you'd like to guv me something for it, sir?

BROWNLOW. *(Aside.)* Yes, that I should — just such another I

BUTCHER. Oh! here cums a policeman.

BROWNLOW. *(Muttering.)* Who generally is the last person who does come on such occasions.

(Enter POLICEMAN.)

POLICEMAN. Come— get up*! (Roughly seizing OLIVER.)*

OLIVER. It wasn't me, indeed. It was two other boys — they are here somewhere.

POLICEMAN. No, no, they ain't.

BROWNLOW. Don't hurt him, officer. D — mn it, sir, I say, don't hurt the boy, or. by the Lord! I'll thrash the dust out of your blue jacket.

BUTCHER. What! ossault a hofficer? Twig his wig and his tail! Oh, what a nice old gentleman!

(The Mob laugh vociferously at MR. BROWNLOW, who is in a fit of indignation, lays lustily about him with his cane, plaguing him m every form and manner ; then with loud hurrahs, drag off OLIVER.)

BUTCHER. Well, but you'll follow and make the charge?

BROWNLOW. Don't hurt the boy, I say. *(Exits.)*

SCENE VI

Interior of a metropolitan police office.

MR. FANG on bench, reading a newspaper — noise and scuffle made by POLICEMEN and Others as they drag in OLIVER — the OFFICER OF THE COURT calls "Silence!" before the bar is thronged with individuals.

OFFICER. Where is the gentleman who makes the charge?

POLICEMAN. He's coming, sir. Make way, there, for the gentleman.

(MR. BROWNLOW enters the office and comes forward. He bows respectfully to the Magistrate's desk, then places his card upon it.)

BROWNLOW. That is my name and address.

(He then withdraws a pace or two, and, making a slight inclination of the head, waits to be questioned.)

FANG. *(Looking from over the paper, and appearing angry at being disturbed, speaks abruptly.)* Who are you?

BROWNLOW. If you'll be kind enough to look at it, my name is on that card; and —

FANG. Officer! *(Tossing away the card, contemptuously.)* Who, fellow?

BROWNLOW. Fellow! fellow! My name is Brownlow. Permit me to inquire the name of the magistrate who offers a gratuitous and unprovoked assault to a respectable man under the protection of the bench?

FANG. Officer! what is this fellow charged with?

OFFICER. He's not charged at all, your worship. He appears against the boy.

FANG. Appears against the boy, does he?— swear him!

BROWNLOW. Before I am sworn. I must beg to say one word, and that is that I never, without actual experience, could have believed—

FANG. Hold your tongue, sir!

BROWNLOW. I will not, sir!

FANG. Hold your tongue this instant, or I'll have you turned out of the office. You're an insolent, impertinent fellow! How dare you bully a magistrate ? Know, sir, that you address a gentleman!

BROWNLOW. 'Tis well you tell me so, sir, for without that information I should never have discovered it.

FANG. Umph ! What is your charge against this boy? What have you got to say?

BROWNLOW. I was standing at a book stall —

FANG. Umph! You flatter yourself that you can read, sir.

BROWNLOW. Yes! I flatter myself I can, sir.

FANG. Silence, sir! Where's the policeman? — at least he is respectable, and I'll listen to him! Are there any witnesses, policeman?

POLICEMAN. None, your worship.

FANG. Now, then, Mr. Low-grown — and low enough no doubt you are — do you mean to give evidence, or do you not? If you do not, I'll punish you for disrespect to the bench — I will, by —

(The CLERK here lets fall a book, and the OFFICER coughs loudly — FANG checks himself.)

BROWNLOW. The fall of that book was fortunate for you, as it has saved you the penalty of an oath.

FANG. Fine me? — a magistrate?

BROWNLOW. Yes, you! D'ye think that laws are made like cobwebs, to catch alone the little flies, and let the greater ones break through? No! and if that word upon the tip of your tongue just now, had found its way from out your mouth, you should have been fined upon your own bench, nor would I have left the office till you had paid it. But I really think the boy is ill.

FANG. Come, none of your tricks here, you young vagabond — they won't do.

OFFICER. But what's to be done with the boy, your worship?

FANG. He stand committed for three months, and of course, hard labor— clear the office.

(The BOOKSELLER enters breathless.)

BOOKSELLER. *(With haste.)* Stop! stop! don't take him away — for heaven's sake stop a moment!

FANG. What is this? Who is this? Clear the office — turn this man out.

BOOKSELLER. I will speak, and I will not be turned out. I keep the book-stall — I saw it all through the window. The robbery was committed by two other boys, and this one here is entirely innocent.

FANG. Umph! why didn't you come here before?

BOOKSELLER Because I could get nobody to mind the shop till five minutes ago.

FANG. And this old suspicious character was reading — was he?

BROWNLOW. Suspicious character! Sir I —

FANG. Silence! He was reading, I say.

BOOKSELLER He was — the very book he has got in his hand.

FANG. Oh! that book, eh! Is it paid for?

BOOKSELLER. No, it is not.

BROWNLOW. Dear me! I forgot all about it.

FANG. I dare say you did — I thought how it would turn out. My good man, do you mean to prosecute the old vagabond?

BROWNLOW. Prosecute me!

FANG. He declines! a most fortunate circumstance in your favor. Now are you not a nice person to prefer a charge against a poor friendless boy— a boy, too, who from the first, my heart and eye told he was laboring under evident indisposition. I consider, sir, that you have obtained possession of that book under very suspicious and disreputable circumstances, and you may think yourself fortunate that the owner of the property declines to prosecute. Let this be a lesson to you, my man, I speak to yon as a friend, and out of compassion; give up this way of life or the law, and perhaps the gallows will overtake you yet — for, possibly, a more grey headed and hardened offender, never appeared before me.

BROWNLOW. Sir — sir — I'll — I shall choke — sir — sir — But the boy — Take care of him, officer, or he'll fall down.

FANG. Stand away, officer, and let him fall if he likes.

(OFFICER does so — the BOY falls.)

BROWNLOW. D — n me, if I didn't say so!

FANG. Fine that fellow for illegal swearing.

(OFFICERS clear the office and turn him out — clamor in which they endeavor to appease MR. BROWNLOW, but in vain — others assisting Oliver. A tableau on which the drop falls.)

End of Act I

ACT II

SCENE I

A parlor in the house of Mr. Brownlow—fireplace on one side, OLIVER seated in an easy chair beside it, a table close to him — portrait of a lady in a conspicuous situation — MRS. BEDWIN stands leaning over Oliver's chair — MR. BROWNLOW in his dressing-gown anxiously gazing at the countenance of OLIVER.

BROWNLOW. And so, Mrs. Bed win, the doctor thinks that with common care he is so far recovered as to go out to-day '?

MRS. BEDWIN. He says so, sir.

OLIVER. How long have I been ill, ma'am?

MRS. BEDWIN. A whole month, my dear.

BROWNLOW. Have you given him any nourishment, Bedwin— any slops?

MRS. BEDWIN. Slops, indeed! he has just had a basin of beautiful broth.

BROWNLOW. Ugh! a couple of glasses of port wine would have done him a great deal more good, wouldn't they Tom White, eh?

OLIVER. My name is Oliver, sir.

BROWNLOW. Oliver what? Oliver White?

OLIVER. Oliver Twist.

BROWNLOW. Twist! queer name— very queer name. *(Musing.)* I can't tell how or why, but the features of that boy seem as familiar to me as — *(His eye is directed to the picture')* Gracious God! what's this — Bedwin, look — look there. *(Pointing to it and then to OLIVER.)* There is its living copy — the eyes — the head — the mouth — so like that. *(Loud knocking heard without.)* Go — go to the door, Bedwin.

(Exit MRS. BEDWIN. He looks at the boy most earnestly.)

OLIVER. Why do you look so closely at me — do you not love me still?

BROWNLOW. I do — I do — but I want you to pay great attention to what I say.

OLIVER. Oh! don't tell me that you are going to send me away, sir! pray don't turn me out of doors to wander in the streets again. Let me stay here and be a servant — don't send me back to the wretched place I came from — have mercy upon a poor boy, sir ; oh, sir! I never will deceive you, never.

BROWNLOW. I do think you never will; still, I have been deceived before in the objects whom I have endeavored to benefit — but I feel disposed to trust you, nevertheless, and am more strongly interested in your behalf than I can well account for, even to myself. The persons on whom I have bestowed my dearest love lie deep in their graves! but though the happiness and delights of my life lie buried there, yet I have not made a coffin of my heart, and on my best affections, sealed it up for ever. Deep affliction has only made them stronger; it ought I think, for it should refine our nature. *(OLIVER sits quite still, deeply attentive to the old gentleman.)* Well, well — I only say this because you have a young heart, and knowing that I have suffered great pain and sorrow, you will be more careful, perhaps, not to wound me again. You say you are an orphan without a friend in the world, and all the inquiries I have been able to make, confirm the tale. Let me hear your story further; where you came from, and who brought you up, and how you got into the company in which I found you — speak the truth, and if I find you have committed no crime, you will never be friendless while I live.

(Enter MRS. BEDWIN.)

MRS. BEDWIN. It's Mr. Grimwig, sir.

BROWNLOW. Is he coming up?

MRS. BEDWIN. Yes, sir! he asked if there were any muffins in the house, and when I told him yes — he said he had come to tea.

BROWNLOW. I shall be glad to see him — say so. *(Exit MRS. BEDWIN.)* An old friend of mine — rough and eccentric — but a good soul at bottom, as well I know.

OLIVER. Shall I go down stairs, sir?

BROWNLOW. No! I would rather you stopped here.

(Exit MR. BROWNLOW. OLIVER goes to sleep — visions appear at back disclosing pictures of his mother's reception at the workhouse, and her death. Scene closes quietly.)

Scene II

A street in Clerkenwell. — A beer-shop, with door in front, forming a prominent feature of it.

Enter MR. SIKES and FAGIN, from left.

FAGIN. He has not peached yet. But if Oliver should tell his new friends, why it is all U P with us, my tere.

SIKES. You mean it is U P with you, Fagin.

FAGIN. Both — all of us, my tere — all of us.

SIKES. And you've found out where the kid is?

FAGIN. He went to the office, and on examination was acquitted — and we've traced him since to an old gentleman's, living at Pentonville.

SIKES. And what's all that to me?

FAGIN. We have a mutual interest, Bill — a mutual interest.

SIKES. Umph! I should think the interest lay more on your side than on mine. Oh, grin away; you'll never have the laugh at me, though — unless it should be behind a nightcap. I've got the upper hand over you, Fagin, and I'll keep it. If I go, you go; so take care on me.

FAGIN. You forget who I am, my tere — you forget who I am.

SIKES. You're an in-sa-ti-a-ble old fence; I wonder they don't murder you. If I'd ha' been one o' your prentices, I'd a done it long ago — and — no, I couldn't have sold you arterwards though, for you're fit for nothing but to keep as a curiosity of ugliness, in a glass bottle, and I suppose they don't blow them large enough.

FAGIN. Hush! hush! Mr. Sikes.

SIKES. None of your mistering. You always mean mischief when you come to that. My name is Bill Sikes, and I shan't disgrace it, when the time comes.

FAGIN. No doubt! But the boy! I've put Nancy upon the scent, and she and you must lure him to the other ken. I've dressed her up like a respectable servant-maid.

SIKES. A dolly-mop, eh, Fagin; and here she comes, with a bonnet, apron, basket, and street door key complete. *(Enter MISS NANCY, arrayed according to the description of Mr. Sikes.)* So, Nancy, you are on the scent, are you?

NANCY. Yes, Bill, I am; and tired enough of it I am too. The young brat has been ill and confined to the crib; and —

FAGIN. I say, Nancy, my tere, I want you to go somewhere for me.

NANCY. Wheres?

FAGIN. To Mr. Brownlow's house, at Pentonville, and inquire for Oliver Twist.

NANCY. I won't go.

FAGIN. But, Nancy! bless my heart, what a pretty creature you are!

NANCY. I know I am. But there — I won't, and it's no use trying it on!

SIKES. What do you mean by that?

NANCY. What I say.

SIKES. Why, you're just the person for it. Nobody about there knows any thing of you.

NANCY. And as I don't want 'em to, neither, it's rather more no than yes, with me.

SIKES. She'll go.

NANCY. No she won't! *(Loudly.)*

SIKES. Yes she will!

NANCY Well! and if I do — to oblige you, Mr. Sikes — what shall I say?

SIKES. Why, if a woman don't know what to say, I'm blowed if I know what to tell 'em.

NANCY. I've got it — I'll say that I am his sister, and that l am looking for my little brother, that has been stoled away. *(With much pathos.)* Oh, my brother! my dear, sweet, innocent little brother! oh, dear!

FAGIN. There; very good — very good, indeed. Ah! you're a clever girl.

SIKES. She's a honor to her sex; and I wish they was all like her.

NANCY. Dye my silk stockings, if it ain't the boy himself a-coming! Sikes, get into the beer-shop — Fagin, get away altogether. *(Pushing FAGIN.)*

FAGIN. I will, my tere.

(SIKES goes into beer-shop. — FAGIN exits left. Enter OLIVER, with books.)

OLIVER. What a change is this! How happy and contented I ought to be. Oh, what would I give if little Dick could see me now. *(Enter a BUTCHER'S BOY.)* Which is the nearest way to the Green, at Clerkenwell?

NANCY. Is it possible — at last I've found him! *(Throws her arms round the neck of OLIVER.)* My brother! my dear brother! Oh! oh! oh!

OLIVER. Don't! Let go of me! Who is it? what are you stopping me for?

(Attracted by the ejaculations of NANCY, enter several PEOPLE right and left.)

NANCY. Oh. my gracious! I've found him! Oh, Oliver! Oh, you naughty boy to make me suffer such distress on your account. Come home, dear, come. Thank gracious heavens I've found him. Oh! oh! oh! *(Falls into the arms of a CARPENTER.)*

WOMEN. Don't you think you had better run for a doctor, butcher?

BUTCHER. No, I don't.

NANCY. Ohl, no, no, no — never mind, I'm better now. *(Grasping OLIVER by the hand.)* Come home, directly, you cruel boy — come —

WOMAN. What's the matter, ma'am?

NANCY. Oh, ma'am, he ran away near a month ago, from his parents, who are hard-working people, and joined a set of bad characters, and almost broke his mother's heart.

WOMEN. Go home, you young wretch, you little brute, you!

OLIVER. I'm not! I don't know her — I haven't got any sister, or father, or mother.

NANCY. Oh, only hear him, how he braves it out!

OLIVER. Why, it's' Nancy.

NANCY. There, you sees he know's me. Make him come home, good people, or he'll kill his poor mother and father, and break my heart!

(Enter SIKES.)

SIKES. What the devil's this? What! young Oliver! come home to your poor mother, you young dog. *(Seizing him.)*

WOMEN. Oh, you shameful child!

OLIVER. I don't belong to them. Oh, let me go! help — help!

SIKES. Help! yes, I'll help you. What books are these? *(Taking them from him.)* Give 'em here!

(Strikes the boy with them on the head.)

WOMEN. That's right. That's the only to bring him to his senses.

SIKES. And he shall have it, too.

NANCY. Good heavens! don't hurt him much, good gentlemen, but take him to his mother. I — I am string to hysterics — I am —

WOMEN. Oh, look at his poor sister!

SIKES. Come along, young rebel.

(SIKES drags off OLIVER. The Mob follows, with MISS NANCY loudly screaming, and apparently in strong hysterics.)

SCENE III

The den of Fagin.

FAGIN discovered sitting in a melancholy mood.

FAGIN. I think Nancy can-not fail; but cost what it may, that boy must, be brought back. *(Scuffle heard on the stairs.)* Eh! they are comins.

SIKES. *(Without.)* Is the old un here?

DODGER. *(Without.)* Yes; and precious down in the mouth he is—won't he be glad to see you!

(Enter SIKES, dragging in OLIVER, followed by NANCY, and preceded by the DODGER and CHARLEY BATES ; the DODGER holding candle in a cleft stick.)

CHARLEY. Oh, my wig! — oh, cry, Fagin, look at him! I can't hear it— ha! ha! — it is such a jolly game. Hold me, somebody, while I laugh it out.

FAGIN. Delighted to see you looking so well, my dear. The Artful shall give you another suit, my dear, for fear you should spoil that Sunday one. Why didn't you write, my dear, to say you were, coming? We'd have got something warm for your supper.

{*The DODGER during this is rifling his pockets with assiduity.)*

DODGER. S'elp me! if there ain't a fi-pun flimsy!

(Holding up note,— FAGIN seizes the note.)

SIKES. Hollo! what's that? That's mine, Fagin.

FAGIN. No, no, my tere, you shall have the books.

SIKES. If that ain't mine, I'll take the boy back again! Come, hand it over.

FAGIN. This is hardly fair — is it, Nancy?

SIKES. Fair, or not fair, hand it over. Do you think Nancy and me has got nothing else to do with our precious time, but to spend it in scouting arter and kidnapping every young boy as gets grabbed through you? Give it here, you avaricious old skeleton! Give it here! *(He snatches it.)* There, you may keep the books, if you are fond of reading; and if not, you can sell 'em.

OLIVER. No, no, they belonged to the old gentleman who took me into the house, and had me nursed when I was dying of the fever. Oh, pray send him back the books and the money! Keep me here all my life long, but send them back, or he'll think I stole them.

FAGIN. You are right — they *will* think you stole them. It couldn't ha' been better.

SIKES In course it couldn't. It's all right enough. They're soft-hearted people, so they'll ask no questions after him, fear they should be obliged to prosecute, and so get him lagged. He's safe enough.

OLIVER. Ah, then! I won't stop if you kill me!

(OLIVER rushes down stairs, followed by the DODGER and BATES.)

FAGIN. If he get away, I am ruined! Yes, Sikes, and so are you.

(Exit FAGIN.)

SIKES. The dog's outside the door, he'll —

(Going to the door — NANCY stands before it.)

NANCY. You shan't set on the dog — he'll tear the boy to pieces.

SIKES. Stand off from me— *(as she clings to him)* — or I'll split your skull against the wall!

NANCY. I don't care for that, Bill! The child shan't be hurt by the dog, unless you first kill me.

(Enter FAGIN and BOYS, with OLIVER.)

SIKES. Shan't he? I'll soon do that if you don't keep off.

FAGIN. What's the matter here?

SIKES. The girl's gone mad.

NANCY. No she hasn't.

SIKES. Then keep quiet.

NANCY. No I won't.

(FAGIN produces a knotted club stick.)

FAGIN. So you wanted to get away, did you? — wanted to call for the police, eh?

(He is about to strike OLIVER a violent blow, when NANCY with a sudden rush, makes herself mistress of the sticky and stands in a protecting attitude over OLIVER.)

NANCY. Now strike the boy if you dare — any of you!

FAGIN. But, Nancy, my tere —

NANCY. Don't dear me! I won't stand by and see it done! You have got the boy, and what more would you have? Let him be then, or I shall put that mark on some on you that will bring me to the gallows before my time!

SIKES. What do you mean? Burn my body! do you know who you are and what you are?

NANCY. Oh, yes! I know all about it — well — well.

(Shaking her head with assumed indifference.)

SIKES. You're a nice un — to take up the humane and genteel side! — a pretty subject for the child to make a friend!

NANCY. God help me! I am! I am! and I wish I had been struck dead in the streets before I had lent a hand in bringing him to where he is. Ah me! He's a thief from this night forth — and isn't that enough without more cruelty!

FAGIN. Civil words.

NANCY. Civil words, Fagin! Do you deserve them from me? Who taught me to pilfer and to steal, when I was a child not half so old as this? — You! I have been -in the trade and in your service twelve years since, and you know it well — you know you do!

FAGIN. And if you have, it is your living.

NANCY. Ah! it is — it is my living! and the cold, wet, dirty streets, are my home! and you're the wretch who drove me to 'em long ago, and that'll keep me there till I die.

FAGIN. I shall do you a mischief — a mischief worse than that — if you say much.

NANCY. Devil!

(She rushes at FAGIN. — SIKES snatches the stick from her., then seizes her waist. — NANCY utters a piercing scream, then, with a look of concentrated hate and horror at FAGIN, she faints in the arms of SIKES.)

SCENE IV

The house of Mrs. Mann. — An interior.

Enter BUMBLE and MRS. MANN.

BUMBLE. Yes, Mrs. Mann, I am going to London — to London, ma'am— 1 and two paupers. A legal action is coming on about a settlement, and the board has appointed me to depose the matter before the Quarter Sessions at Clerkenwell; and I very much question if the Clerkenwell Sessions will not find themselves in the wrong box before they have done with me.

MRS. MANN. Oh, you mustn't be too hard upon them.

BUMBLE. They brot it upon themselves, and if the Clerkenwell Sessions find that they come off rather worse than they expected, the Clerkenwell Sessions have only themselves to thank.

MRS. MANN. Are you going by coach, Mr. Bumble!

BUMBLE. I am — inside, Mrs. Mann, with my face to the horses, for if I ride with my back to 'em, Mrs. Mann, such is the delicacy of my constitution, that in general it makes me vomix.

MRS. MANN. You're going by coach; but I thought it was usual to send the paupers in carts.

BUMBLE. That's when they're ill, and then we put the sick paupers into open carts, to prevent their catching cold. The opposition coach contracts for these two, and takes them cheap. They are both in a very low state, and we find it would come two pound cheaper to move 'em than to bury 'em; that is if we can throw 'em upon another parish, which I think we shall be able to do, if they don't die upon the road to spite us. But how are the orphans under your porochiall care, Mrs. Mann?

MRS. MANN. All well, Mr. Bumble, I thank you, but little Dick.

BUMBLE. What! isn't he dead yet?

MRS. MANN. Not yet. Ah! poor little boy, he does go on so, and talks so much about that runaway prentice, Oliver Twist.

BUMBLE. Talking of that, here's the London paper; I borrowed it just to show you this nacknack from it. *(Reads.)* "Five guineas reward. Whereas a young boy, named Oliver Twist, absconded or was enticed on Thursday evening last from his home at Pentonville; the above reward will be paid to any person who will give such information as to lead to his discovery, or tend to throw any light upon his previous history, in which the advertiser is for many reasons warmly interested." Now, Mrs. Mann, I should think no person more fitter than myself could be found to give such information; so good bye, Mrs. Mann.

MRS. MANN. Good bye, Mr. Bumble; and I hope your merits will meet their due reward.

BUMBLE. And if so, them five guineas will find themselves as safe as the bank in my porochial pocket.

(Exeunt severally, BUMBLE, left, and MRS. MANN, right.)

Scene V

Repetition of Scene the First.

MR. BROWNLOW and MR. GRIMWIG, with decanters before them, over their wine.

BROWNLOW. Heigho!

GRIMWIG. Ah, you may well sigh; you'll have more to sigh for, Mr. B., depend on't, before this affair is over. If you don't, sir, I'll eat my head. You've advertised for the young ruffian, you say?

BROWNLOW. As yet without success.

GRIMWIG. Umph! so much the better — you wouldn't like to see him hanged, would you?

BROWNLOW. Good heavens, no!

GRIMWIG. Then avoid passing debtor's door when you go near the Old Bailey.

(Enter MRS. BEDWIN hastily.)

MRS. BEDWIN. I knew we should hear of him, poor dear — I knew we should — I was certain of it — I said so all along.

BROWNLOW. Thank God! thank God!

MRS. BEDWIN. Excuse my crying — but — oh — dear — oh dear I am so glad!

BROWNLOW. Mrs. Bedwin — Mrs.— *(Puts kerchief to his nose.)*Pooh! I'm a d—d old fool!

GRIMWIG. Why, what's the matter, my good friend?— you seem a little hoarse.

BROWNLOW. Yes; I'm afraid, Mrs. Bedwin, you didn't sufficiently air the cravat I put on this morning.

MRS. BEDWIN. Yes, Mr. Brownlow, that I did; but there's a person below who says he can tell us something about Oliver.

BROWNLOW. Tell him to come up directly.

MRS. BEDWIN. You may come up.

(Enter MR. BUMBLE — he bows to the two gentlemen in a most respectful manner — BUMBLE wears a great-coat.)

GRIMWIG. I see it by his waddle — a parish beadle — or I'll eat my head.

BROWNLOW. Sit down, sir.

BUMBLE. I will, sir. *(Sitting.)*

BROWNLOW. Will you take a glass of wine?

BUMBLE. I will, sir. *(Drinking.)* Your healths, gentlemen, both.

BROWNLOW. Now, sir. You come in consequence of having seen an advertisement?

GRIMWIG.. *(Quickly.)* And you are a beadle — are you not?

BUMBLE. Yes — a porochial beadle.

GRIMWIG. Of course! I said he was. His coat has a porochial cut all over. If he hadn't been a beadle, I'd have eat my own head, and his afterwards!

BUMBLE. *(Aside.)* Would you? Then, to my thinking, there would be more brains in your belly than in all the upper part of your body!

BROWNLOW. My friend, do you know where this poor boy is now?

BUMBLE. No more than nobody.

BROWNLOW. Well, what do you know of him? Speak out, if you've any thing to say.

GRIMWIG. You don't happen to know any good of him, do you?

BUMBLE. *(Aside.)* I wonder which I shall get most by — by blowing him up, or praising him?

GRIMWIG. Of course you don't know any good of him?

BUMBLE. *(Aside.)* Oh, that's my cue! — Of course I don't.

BROWNLOW. Speak, then, sir — you can speak?

BUMBLE. Sir, you wound my feelings. Yes, sir, I can speak, and sing too. 'Tis plain, sir, that you was never at Mudfoor church during service — *(with increased vehemence and insulted dignity)* — or you would never have asked the question, sir. I'd have you to know I sing the psalms louder than six people put together, and, if the charity-boy didn't blow the bellows very strong, I should drown the organ!

GRIMWIG. There, there — that will do.

BUMBLE. I tell you, sir, that it won't do. I'd have you to know that my voice is 'ticklary fine! Lor, sir — the voice of the beadle is the wox populi of the parish, the engine of the overseer, and the terror of the pauporial population, No voice, sir — no voice! — allow me to exalt it, and I'll make those decanters upon the table shake as if they had got the ague, and rattle the tiles upon the top of the house in such a manner, that the chimney-pots will be astonished! *(Singing.)* Good people, listen!

BROWNLOW. Get down sir! — get down! *(For BUMBLE, in his excitement has mounted the chair.)*

GRIMWIG. Yes, get down— or I'll eat my head if I don't make you.

BUMBLE. Beg your pardon — but I forgot. *(Sitting down.)*

BROWNLOW. Oliver Twist — what know you of Oliver Twist 1

BUMBLE. The sums substance is, that he was a foundling — born of lewd, vicious parents. From his birth he was treacherous, ungrateful, and malicious. In a word, he nearly killed an unoffending boy, called Noah Claypole, and finished by running away in the night- time from his master's house, who was almost a father to him.

BROWNLOW. Indeed! indeed!

GRIMWIG. I said so all along.

BROWNLOW. And who are you?

BUMBLE. I am the Beadle of the parish in which he was born, sir.

BROWNLOW. There, then, is the five guineas. If your conscience would have permitted you to have given him a more favorable account, I should have made them ten, sir,

BUMBLE. Weugh! I've put both foots in it. But, sir —

BROWNLOW. Have you more to say of Oliver Twist?

BUMBLE. No — but —

BROWNLOW. There is the door. You will excuse me, but your society at this moment is any thing but pleasant.

BUMBLE. But, sir —

BROWNLOW. Begone, sir!

BUMBLE. What a fiery old dragon! I wish I had him for a few minutes under the spout of our porochial pump — egad. I'd cool his courage. *(Exits.)*

BROWNLOW. Heigho! so Oliver is an impostor.

MRS. BEDWIN. It can't be!

BROWNLOW. What do you mean by it can't be?— I tell you he is.

MRS. BEDWIN. I won't believe it.

GRIMWIG. You old women never believe anybody but quack doctors.

MRS. BEDWIN. You are an old bachelor; and people who never had no children ought not to give no opinion.

BROWNLOW. Silence! Never let me hear that boy's name again, on any pretense. I am in earnest. Remember! Good night, my friend.

GRIMWIG. Good night. *(Exits.)*

BROWNLOW. My bed candle.

MRS. BEDWIN. 'Tis here, sir. *(Giving it him.)*

BROWNLOW. Go!

MRS. BEDWIN. *(Crying.)* Oh, lackaday! Oh, lackaday! *(Exits.)*

(MR. BROWNLOW, after a pause, sighs heavily and exits to his chamber.)

SCENE VI

FAGING'S den.

Enter Sikes, smoking:, with FAGIN and NANCY— NANCY draws a chair. sitting motionless and listlessly upon it.

FAGIN. About the crib at Chertsen, Bill? — such plate, my tere — such plate!

SIKES. It is not to be done at all. At least, it can't be a put-up job, as we expected.

FAGIN. Then it hasn't been properly gone about. Don't tell me!

SIKES. But I will tell you! Who are you that are not to be told? I say that Tobey Crackit has been hanging about the place for a fortnight, and he can't get one of the servants into a line.

FAGIN. Do you mean to say that neither of the men in the house can be got over?

SIKES. I do.

FAGIN. Nor the women?

SIKES. Not a bit of it.

FAGIN. Not by flash Toby Crackit? — Think what women are!

SIKES. No; not even by flash Toby Crackit!

FAGIN. Tere, tere — 'tis a sad thing to lose so much when we had set our hearts upon it.

SIKES. And so it's, worse luck, Fagin! *(Suddenly.)* Is it worth fifty shiners if it's safely done from the outside instead of the in?

FAGIN. Yes, yes, my tere.

SIKES. Then let it come off as soon as you like. Tobey and I were over the garden- wall the night afore last, sounding the panels of the doors and shutters. There is one part we can crack safely.

FAGIN. And which is that?

Sikes. Never mind which part it is — you can't do without me, I know. But it's best to be on the safe side when one deals with you.

FAGIN. As you likes, my tere — as you likes.

SIKES. One thing we shall need, and you can help us to it — we want a boy. Now, if I had got that young boy o' Ned's, the chimney-sweeper — he kept him small on purpose, and let him out by the job. But the father gets laged, and the Juvenile Delinquent S'iety takes away the boy from a trade where he was arning money, teaches him to read and write, and ruins him! And so they go on. Ah, them charity s'ieties does a deal o' harm! and if they got money enough (which 'tis a providence they ha' not) we wouldn't have a spectable boy-thief in all London.

FAGIN. No more we should. But, I say Bill, don't you talk too fast. *(Pointing to NANCY.)*

SIKES. Pooh! she won't blab — will you, Nance?

NANCY. I should think not. You going to recommend young Oliver — I know you are!

FAGIN. Why my tere, I—I—

NANCY. There, don't stammer, tell Sikes at once. Remember, Fagin, you and I can't call each other strangers. We — we know each other!

FAGIN. It was about Oliver I was going to speak, sure enough. He's the boy for you, Sikes.

SIKES. He's just the size —

FAGIN. And will do everything you want — that is, if you'll frighten him!

SIKES. Frighten him! Mark my words, if there's anything queer about him when once we get into the work, you won't see him alive again — so think of it.

FAGIN. I've thought of it all. I've had my eyes upon him close. Once let him feel that he is one of us — once let him think that he has been a thief — and he is ours!

SIKES. What?

FAGIN. Or the poor little boy must be put out of the way, Mr. Sikes.

NANCY. You're a great rogue, Fagin! But I've told you that so often, you cannot have forgotten it.

FAGIN. But when is it to be done?

SIKES. I planned with Toby to-morrow night, if he heard nothing from me to the contrary. The day is breaking. I've hired a cart and horse near by on spec, and shall be off the stones in an hour or two But the boy — where is he? I must have him now or never!

FAGIN. There— sound asleep! So sound that you might put him into the cart without his waking.

SIKES. Oho! oho! Softly!

(Exit SIKES it fetch OLIVER.)

FAGIN. Ha! ha! Good! good! Excellent!— he sleeps so soundly.

NANCY. *(Calmly.)* Do you ever do so, Fagin?

FAGIN. No! Sometimes I dream, my tere— sometimes I dream.

NANCY. Of what?

FAGIN. One night of one thing, and another night of another.

NANCY. One night of your gold, and another of the devil, to whom you sold your soul to gain it. *(Enter SIKES bearing the sleeping OLIVER.)* Stop, Bill, before he goes — let me see him.

(SIKES stops for a moment. — She gazes in the face of OLIVER then bursts into tears.

FAGIN. Eh, why do you cry, my tere?

NANCY. I had a brother about his age that look'd like him in his coffin.

SIKES. Come — come.

(Exit SIKES — FAGIN detaining her for a moment.)

NANCY. What do you stop me for?

FAGIN. You won't betray me?

(FAGIN holds the candle close to her face.)

NANCY. No. *(Boldly.)* What do you stare in my face for?

FAGIN. I'm a judge of faces.

NANCY. Then I tell you again, I won't.

FAGIN. I see by your face you won't — good night.

NANCY. Good night. *(Exits.)*

FAGIN. Umph! she's smooth and fair again. The worst of these women is, that a very little thing serves to call up some long-forgotten feeling, and the best of them is, that it lasts only for a moment. Aha! aha! this is a strange world! How long will it be before I leave it! I — I'll try to pray to-night.

(Exit FAGIN, right.)

Scene VII

A solitary house, by moonlight, ruinous and decayed. — Window on each side of dilapidated entrance, viz.: a low portico. — the door of the portico practicable.

Enter from the doorway TOBY CRACKIT smoking a long clay pipe.

TOBY. *(Calling.)* Barney!

BARNEY. *(Without.)* I'm coming, Master Toby.

TOBY. Well? *(After taking along whiff at pipe.)* 'Tis a surprising thing to me, any how, that people can be honest. For a fortnight have I been down in this here place and havn't come the caper in a shipshape fashun yet. *(Shrill whistle without.)* Who goes there?

SIKES. *(Without.)* What's o'clock? That's the question.

TOBY. Time for to get up early! That's the answer — all right — 'tis Sikes and the boy. Barney, get all ripe and ready.

(Enter SIKES, following OLIVER, right.)

SIKES. Get on — or do you want me to tread upon your heels every minute?

TOBY. Your hand, Bill, I'm glad to do the civil to you.

SIKES. How do you get on?

TOBY. All correct, like a house a-fire at both ends and in the middle.

SIKES. The crack is safe, then.

TOBY. Safe as sawdust, and I'm glad to see you. I was almost afraid you'd given it up, in which case I should have made a personal wentur.

SIKES. Here, Barney, the max.

(Enter BARNEY from the house with waiter, jug of hot water and spirits, yawning.)

TOBY. *(Mixing , and helping SIKES.)* Ah! this will give me a heart now. *(Drinks.)*

OLIVER. Lor! hadn't you a heart before, sir?

TOBY. No — not much of a one. Bill, give the boy a drain of gin,

SIKES. *(Gives the boy a drop of gin.)* Down with it, innocence.

OLIVER. Indeed! I—

TOBY. Tell him to drink it, Bill.

SIKES. He had better.

(Pointing to the handle of his pistol in pocket. — OLIVER drinks it.)

TOBY. There's a gentleman. Now, oh, stop, where's the timber? *(BARNEY offer's two bludgeons, then exits into house.)* Take your choice. Bill — I think this is rather the thickest.

SIKES. This is the sapling. *(Taking one of the bludgeons.)* Which way shall we go?

TOBY. Slap through the town of Chertsey — there'll be nobody in the way to-night to see us. *(To OLIVER.)* I s'pose if it came to the worst, you wouldn't split — for if I thought that, I'd —

OLIVER. No, no! I'll never split, if you don't knock me to pieces.

SIKES. Be as bold as brass, boy.

TOBY. And the moment the devil tempts you to trust to your heels— *(taking hold of Oliver's hand)*— think of this cudgel on one side of you. *(Stretching cudgel out.)*

SIKES. And this on the other. *(Imitating the action of Toby.)*

TOBY. Come, Bill, come; he'll be a rare fellow yet, depend on't, and so to business — to business.

(Exeunt SIKES and TOBY CRACKIT conducting off OLIVER.)

Scene VIII

A building for the purpose of brewing at the back of a house of genteel appearance. In flat a wall practicable forming the boundary of a garden. A small open window sufficiently large to allow the passage of a boy through it, apparent without the brew-house. The morning perfectly dark.

Sikes with his lantern appears above the wall.

SIKES. 'Tis all correct. *(Jumps down.)* Hand the boy over. *(TOBY CRACKIT here shows himself above, and holding OLIVER under the arms, lets him fall into those of SIKES, who catches him.)* Now, Toby, jump, it isn't no distance.

(TOBY jumps down.)

OLIVER. I see it now; robbery, housebreaking, and perhaps murder! *(To TOBY.)* Oh! pray have mercy on me, and do not make me steal.

TOBY. The boy'll split. I'll — *(Cocking his pistol.)*

SIKES. *(To OLIVER.)* Hush! if you do you may count yourself as dead.

OLIVER. What would you have done?

SIKES. Be quiet till I've took down the shutter. *(With a crowbar, and with very little resistance to it, he removes the shutter.)* Now listen, you young limb. *(Throwing light of lantern full on the face of OLIVER.)* I'm going to put you in there. *(Pointing to hall.)* Take this light and go softly up the steps afore you till you come to the street door, and then unfasten it and let us in.

TOBY. There's a bolt at the top, you won't be able to reach, stand upon one of the hall chairs, there are three of 'em with —

SIKES. *(To TOBY who has climbed up with both hands.)* But are you sure the room door's open?

TOBY. Well! The game of that is that they always leave it open with a catch, so that the dog, who has got a bed in here, may walk up and down the passage when he feels wakeful. But he's not there now, Barney 'ticed him away so neat.

SIKES. Kip — *(TOBY plants himself firmly with his head against the wall, beneath the window, and his hands upon his knees, to make a step of his back; SIKES mounts upon him, puts OLIVER gently through the window, with his feet first, and without leaving hold of his collar plants him safely on the floor inside.)* Take this lantern, you see the steps afore you; take notice, you are within shot of this. *(Pointing pistol through embrasure.)* And if you falter, I'll shoot you dead. Lor! 'tis done in a minute.

TOBY. D'ye see the boy? *(Listening at the street door.)*

SIKES. All's right, he goes straight to the door.

(TOBY listens at street door.)

TOBY. What's that? I hear something.

SIKES. Come back, come back. *(Music. — A pistol-shot is heard within. OLIVER utters a cry.)* It's all up; there's another to scare ye.

(OLIVER staggers and falls. Enter from house MR. BROWNLOW, MRS. BEDWIN with SERVANTS and lights.)

BROWNLOW. I hope I have not killed him!

MRS.BEDWIN. Why, 'tis Oliver!

BROWNLOW. Raise him, I say; Mrs. Bedwin, damn it, do something!

(TOBY and SIKES make their escape over wall; and curtain falls on tableau.)

End of Act II

ACT III

Scene I

The Workhouse Parlor,

BUMBLE discovered seated at table, in plain clothing and gazing ruefully on his beadle's coat.

Bumle. I have touched the summum bonum of all porochiat greatness— I am master of the workhouse — I have married a woman whom I like — no — damn it — whom I don't like — and— oh, blessed relics of departed grandeur! 'Tis true I wear a pair of breeches on my nether limbs, but not the breeches— I wear too, a wide skirted coat, but not the coat. There are some promotions in life which acquire peculiar value from the coats and waistcoats connected with them. A field-marshal has his uniform, a bishop, his silk apron, a beadle, his cocked hat — strip the bishop of his apron, or the beadle of his cocked hat, and what are they? — men, mere men! for dignity is often a question more of coat and waistcoat than many people imagen. I must put away these in case they should make me weep, for I am no longer what I was, -and the blessed days of singlehood and beadleism are faded away forever. *(Singing as he puts away the clothes.)* "The light of other days are faded." I have been married about eight weeks, and it seems to me a hundred years, or to speak more properly, a centurion, and I sold myself for six teaspoons, a pair of sugar-tongs, and a milk-pot; with a small quantity of second hand furniture — I went very reasonable — dirt cheap!

(Enter MRS. BUMBLE.)

MRS. BUMBLE. Cheap! cheap! — You would have been dear at any price.

BUMBLE. Mrs. Bumble!

MRS. BUMBLE. Well?

BUMBLE. Have the goodness to look at me! If she stands such an eye as this — an eye that I never new to fail with porochial paupers, she will stand anything and my power is gone forever ! Woman!

(Eyeing her sternly.)

MRS. BUMBLE. Well, booby?

BUMBLE. I am seized with an artepluck agitation, or to speak more properly, a fit of apoplexy.

MRS. BUMBLE. Come, get up, get up — and don't sit snoring there, all day, Mr. Bumble!

BUMBLE. I am going to sit here as long as I think proper— I shall snore, gape, sneeze, laugh, or cry, as the humor suits me — such being my prerogative, as a lord of the creation!

MRS. BUMBLE. You a lord of the creation! I'll have no such whimsy whamies, and you shan't create with me, depend upon it.

BUMBLE. But I will, and a precious riot, Mrs. Bumble. *(Raising his cane.)*

MRS. BUMBLE. What! strike a woman! Oh! you monster!

(Music. — She attacks him, pulls off his wig, and beats him. Enter MONKS, hastily in a walking cloak.)

MONKS. How is this? Is it possible that I behold a wife chastising her husband?

BUMBLE. Chastising! Oh, how shall I eradicate myself from this ignominious situation. Uraph! I dare say it appeared to you that my wife was beating me well.

MONKS. Yes; very well!

BUMBLE. Yes; I feel as if you thought so;

MONKS. I have little doubt you do.

BUMBLE. Ha! ha! ha! Circumstances sometimes areas deceptious as an occulous delusion. Umph! As Mrs. Bumble is getting what in Latin we call ting-bong-poing or to speak more properly—fat.

MRS. BUMBLE. Fat! you villain!

BUMBLE. Not too fat, my love; only a little crummy — and the poroclrial duties requiring her to lead a sequestrated and sedentary life — for her health's sake, I was indulging her with a little exercise this morning.

MONKS. Oh! is that all!

BUMBLE. Oh, yes; that's all, and quite a plenty. Wheugh! what a tongue! I'm afraid Mrs. B. has broken the pulmonary bone of my right arm into decimal fractions.

MONKS. Last night we drank together.

BUMBLE. We did! Six glasses of gin-and-water warm, with sugar. *(Aside.)* This is the man I told you of, who wanted to pump me about the secret — Mrs. Bumble, Mr. Monks. Mrs. Monks — no, I mean — Mrs. Bumble, Mr. Monks, Mrs. Bumble!

MONKS. Oh! this is your good lady!

BUMBLE. Yes I and a good strong lady she is. I am afraid she has broken the corrupted artery of my spinal backbone in a variety of places.

MONKS. *(To BUMBLE.)* You know I can explain my business.

BUMBLE. This gentleman wants to distort a secret from us lovee.

MRS. BUMBLE. Perhaps the gentleman thinks that woman cannot keep a secret?

MONKS. I know they will always keep one, till it is found out.

BUMBLE. One! and what is that?

MONKS. The loss of their own good name. Do you understand me?

MRS. BUMBLE. Understand you? — no, not I!

MONKS. Of course you don't — how should you? Carry your memory back to that spot in the workhouse, where misery gives birth to puling children, for the parish to rear upon its stinted charity.

BUMBLE. You mean the lying-in-room.

MONKS. A boy was born there.

BUMBLE. Ah! a great many boys was born there, in a most illegitimous and unporochial manner.

MONKS. I come to inquire of one — Oliver Twist!

BUMBLE. Of Oliver Twisf? One of the most obstinatest and most deceitfulest —

MONKS. His mother died in the workhouse at his birth; and there was a hag, I think, who nursed her.

BUMBLE. A hag to be sure there was; you nursed her, didn't you, lovee?

MRS. BUMBLE. I, Mr. Bumble! no, not I ; it was Old Sally!

MONKS. And where's old Sally?

BUMBLE. Old Sally, I suspect, is dead.

MONKS. Suspect! and for what reason?

BUMBLE. Oh, for no particular reason, only that I saw her buried.

MRS. BUMBLE. I saw her die.

MONKS. She told you something about the boy's mother!

MRS. BUMBLE. She did.

MONKS. This bag contains the sum of twenty pounds; if you'll tell me the particulars of that old woman's death, I'll give it you.

MRS. BUMBLE. Will you, indeed? Well then, you must know that Old Sally spoke of a young creature who had brought a child into the world before, not merely in the same room, but in the same bed in which she then lay dying. This girl, old Sally confessed to have robbed of a small parcel I took from her clutched hand when dead, and which I myself, in general, carry about with me. Yes, here it is;

(MONKS snatches it.)

MONKS. It contains what?

MRS. BUMBLE. A small locket, with the name of Agnes engraved inside, and a wedding ring.

MONKS. It is — it is the thing I want. (Going.)

BUMBLE. Yes, but whereas the twenty pounds we want?

MONKS. *(Throwing it down.)* There it is! *(Exits.)*

(BUMBLE picks it up.)

MRS. BUMBLE. What are you going to do with that money Mr. Bumble?

BUMBLE. I am going to put it in my porochial pocket!

MRS. BUMBLE. *(Snatches it.)* Give it me! for I'm not only master and mistress, but also cashier to the workhouse. *(Exits.)*

BUMBLE. Cash here! I think it is cash there! She will call herself next the Lord Chanticleer of Exchequer, for preciously she crows over me. "The light of other days is faded."

(Exits, singing mournfully.)

Scene II

A street by moonlight.

Enter MONKS.

MONKS. I have thrown the tokens of the locket and the ring into a mill-stream near at hand; and if the sea ever gives up its dead, as books say it will, it will keep its gold and silver to itself, and that trash among it. But here are papers I fear almost to carry about my person, in case they should be found. *(Enter FAGIN, and listens.)* And, rambler as I am, I have no house or place to hide them in!

FAGIN. *(Coming forward.)* Give them to me, my tere.

(NANCY, who has been following FAGIN, enters, and on seeing who is with him, conceals herself.)

MONKS. Give them to you; and why, Fagin?

FAGIN. For security.

MONKS. For security?

FAGIN. Yes, my tere; for their own security and mine. They will be much safer at my house. I will secrete them in a hole of a dark chimney where we never keep a fire!

MONKS. True! that will be for their security. But what do you mean when you speak of yours?

FAGIN. When the job is completed, and I have done what you would have me do with Oliver, you promised me £500. Put the papers, then, into my hand, that I may be sure, my tere, that you will keep your promise.

MONKS. Be it so! *(Giving them.)* I have been lingering in this cold street these two hours. Where the devil, Fagin, have you been?

FAGIN. About your business, my tere — about your business!

MONKS. You promised me by this time to have made him a pick-pocket, got him convicted and sent out of the country.

FAGIN. But, my tere, he was so obstinate, and wouldn't take kindly to the profession, or he'd been a thief, long, long ago!

MONKS. Pshaw! you have made thieves of other boys in half the time.

FAGIN. True, my tere, but they were half thieves already. Now, the honesty and obstinacy of this boy is disgraceful. But about the other proofs we talked of last night — the locket and the ring?

MONKS. Those proofs of the boy's identity lie at the bottom of the river, and the old hag that received them from his mother, Agnes, is rotting in her coffin. Oh, Fagin! if I could gratify my hatred by taking that boy's life without the loss of my own, I could give you reasons strong for doing it; but I'll be upon the watch to meet him at every turn of life, to short, not even you yourself ever laid such snares as I'll contrive for my young brother Oliver!

NANCY. His brother! *(Exits.)*

MONKS. We have been watched — I caught the shadow of a woman's form on yonder wall. Quick! By this way I will go! *(Exits right.)*

FAGIN. And I by the other! *(Exits left.)*

Scene III

The garret of Sikes.

Sikes discovered lying on bed wrapped in a white great- coat, a soiled nightcap, and a black beard of a week's growth — Seated by him is NANCY, patching an old waist-coat.

NANCY. *(Kissing his lips.)* He is better and stronger now, thank heaven! I have seen the good kind lady, Miss Maylie, and have warned her of the danger threatening Oliver, but without implicating hi —*(pointing to Sikes)*— or others. Let me think! How was my promise worded?— that should they wish to find me, come what might, I would, every Sunday night, be on London-bridge from the hour of eleven till midnight!

SIKES. *(Starting from his sleep.)* Who's there? Bar! bar the door! Oh! it's only you — what's o'clock, Nancy?

NANCY. Near upon ten. How do you feel to-night?

SIKES. As weak as water! Here, lend us a hand, and let us get off this thundering bed any how — do you hear?

NANCY. Don't be cross, now — it's not in your nature!

SIKES. Arn't it, though?

NANCY. You wouldn't — no, I'm sure you wouldn't be hard upon me to-night.

SIKES. No! — and why not?

NANCY. *(Placing her hand on his shoulder and looking in his face.)* Such a number of nights as I've been patient with you, nursing and caring for you as if you had been a child — and this, the first that I have seen you like yourself — Come, come, you wouldn't have served me as you did just now if you'd have thought of that, would you? Say you wouldn't?

SIKES. Well, then, I wouldn't. *(She bursts into tears.)* Well! — why, what are you whining about now, Nancy?

NANCY. Don't — don't seem to mind me! It will soon be over!

SIKES. What'll soon be over? Get up and bustle about, and don't becoming over me with your woman's nonsense. *(Knocking.)* Who's there? *(Three low taps.)* Three low taps! Then 'tis one of us. Come in, whoever you be!

(Enter FAGIN followed by the DODGER and BATES. The Dodger with basket of provisions.)

FAGIN. Oh, Bill, my tere! — how do you do?

SIKES. Not much the better for seeing you!

FAGIN. Aha! but you'll b« the better for what we've brought. Spread the drapery, Nance!

(Handing table-cloth, NANCY spreads it — he takes out from basket knives; forks etc.)

SIKES. Umph! Have you got anything there to eat?

DODGER. Look here, Bill! Sitch a rabbit-pie! Sitch delicate creturs, with sitch tender limbs that the very bones melt in your mouth, and there's no occasion to pick 'em; half a pound o' seven-and-six- penny gunpowder-tea, so precious strong, that if you mix it with boiling water it'll go nigh to blow the lid o' the teapot off; a pound an' a half o' mist sugar, that the niggers didn't work at at all aforo they got it to sitch a pitch o' goodness — oh, no! Two half-quartern brans — pound o' best fresh — piece of double Gloucester — and, to wind up all, some of the richest port you ever lushed! *(Filling a glass and handing it to SIKES, who swallows the contents.)* That's the stuff for trowsers, ar'nt it, Bill? — so strong that it would make a man drunk only to pass by the cask it was kept in!

SIKES. Give us another!— I arn't hardly got at the right taste !

DODGER. Enquivore! as I used to say in the gallery when I used to go and see Jim Crow, just to encourage the legitimate drammy!

FAGIN. Aha! you'll do. Bill, now — you'll do!

SIKES. Do 1 — I might have been done for twenty times over afore you'd ha' done anything to help me! What do you mean by leaving a man in this state three weeks or more, you false-hearted vagabond?

FAGIN. Only hear him, boys — only hear him! And us to come and brings him such beautiful things!

SIKES. And what made you keep away for, you withered old fence?

FAGIN. I couldn't help it, Bill—I couldn't, on my honor!

SIKES. Upon your what? — Here, somebody cut us off a bit o' pie, to take the taste o' that out o' my mouth, or it will choke me!

FAGIN. Don't be out of temper— I have never forgot you, Bill.

SIKES. No! I'll pound it you haven't. You've been scheming and plotting away every hour that I've laid shivering and burning here. If it hadn't been for the girl I might have died. Well, well, I must have some blunt from you to-night.

FAGIN. I hav'n't a coin about me.

SIKES. Then you've got lots at home.

FAGIN. Lots! — I hav'n't got so much as —

SIKES. I don't want to know how much you've got, and I dare say you couldn't tell yourself as it would take a pretty long time to count it. But I must have some to-night, and that's flat, Fagin!

FAGIN. I'll send the Artful! Here, Artful! there's the key of the drawer — you know where. In a corner of it you'll find seven shillings.

NANCY. What's o'clock?

FAGIN. Near upon twelve.

NANCY. Near twelve! My promise, my promise! I'll go for the money.

SIKES. Stay where you are! And, d'yo hear, Dodger — Artful don't be too artful for me!

DODGER. What do you mean? I'm sure I'd never deceive a friend — unless he'd let me!

SIKES. Then don't lose your way coming back with the ready, or be dodged by the traps, or —

DODGER. Or have a hole in my pocket, or spend it by mistake, a' thinking it was my own, or lend it to a friend, or have my feelings touched and give it to a beggar — or — oh! strike me backwards! take my arm. Charley, and let us get away from this here gentleman, for of all the horridness weaknesses of human nature, there's nothing what can ever give up to a suppositious disposition !

SIKES. Oh! you're a nice young gentleman!

DODGER. Yes, we just am, and there's a pair on us! And, for the future, Mr. Sikes, I beg you won't touch your hat to us in the street, cos as how we cuts your company!

(Exeunt Boy, swaggering, NANCY following.)

SIKES. What, Nance! Nancy, I say! Where's the gal going, eh?

NANCY. I don't know where.

SIKES. Then I can tell you — nowhere! So sit down.

NANCY. *(Aside.)* 'Tis near the time. I want a breath of air.

SIKES. Then put your head out o' the winder,

NANCY. That's not enough — I want it in the street!

SIKES. Then you won't have it! *(Snatching her bonnet.)* There, now, stop quietly where you are!

NANCY. It isn't such a matter as a bonnet would keep me. Do you know what you are doing?

SIKES. Know what I'm doing? the girl's lost her senses. Know what I'm doing! Yes, holding you down in this ere chair.

NANCY. You'll drive me on to something desperate! Tell him to let me go, Fagin — this minute! this instant!

FAGIN. I, my tere? — I never interfere. *(Aside.)* If they quarrel the better for me!

NANCY. *(Aside.)* My promise made to be on London Bridge. Oh! let me go! if only for an hour, one hour!

FAGIN. Good-night! 'Tis about striking twelve. Good-night! Good night. *(Aside.)* If they quarrel and separate, they are mine together.

NANCY. Fagin! dear Fagin! take me with you!

FAGIN. I cannot, my tere — I cannot. *(Exits.)*

NANCY. *(Kneeling.)* Oh, let me go; if you ever loved me —

SIKES. Cut my limbs off one by one, if the girl isn't raving mad.

NANCY. Let me go! let me go!

(Clock strikes twelve.)

SIKES. Twelve o'clock; there, don't you hear! *(She screams.)* What are you screaming for? There, go if you will.

NANCY. I don't want to go now. *(Aside.)* I have broken my promise, and the time is over.

(Music. — Falls insensible on the bed.)

End of Act III

ACT IV

Scene 1

London Bridge.

Music. Enter NANCY, conducting ROSE and BROWNLOW.

ROSE. You were not here, last Sunday night?

NANCY. I couldn't come — he kept me at home by force.

BROWNLOW. Who kept you at home?

NANCY. Bill! the man I told the lady of.

ROSE. Heard you no more of the other one, called Monks?

NANCY. Yes, I heard Monks say that Oliver was the child he had long been watching for, though I couldn't tell why; but a bargain was struck with Fagin to make Oliver a thief— which this Monks was anxious for, to further some purpose of his own.

BROWNLOW. And for what purpose, girl?

NANCY. He caught sight of my shadow on the wall as I listened in the hope of finding it out; but I couldn't — no, I couldn't. But I heard him say to Fagin, this — that Jew as you are, you never laid such snares as I'll contrive for my young brother, Oliver!

ROSE. His brother! Gracious heavens!

NANCY. Aye; thank heaven on your knees, that you had friends to care for, and keep you in your childhood; and that were never in the midst of cold, and hunger, and riot, and drunkenness, and something worse, as I have been from my cradle! — ah! I may use the word! for the alley and the gutter were my cradle, as they will be my death-bed.

BROWNLOW. You were not suspected of holding communication with anybody on the subject which has brought us here to-night?

NANCY. No, it is not easy for me to leave without his knowledge; nor could I when I did, but that I gave him a drink of laudanum before I came away.

BROWNLOW. Now listen to me!

NANCY. I am ready.

BROWNLOW. I think we can extort the secret from the fears of this man, Monks.

NANCY. There are certain papers hid where I think I can come at them, that may serve you much; and if I live so long, they shall be yours to-morrow.

BROWNLOW. Thank you, my good girl. But if he cannot be secured you must deliver up the Jew!

NANCY. I'll not do it devil that he is, and worse than devil that he has been to me, that I will never do!

BROWNLOW. Where do you think it likely we may meet with this Monks?

NANCY. I have scrawled his haunts down on this fragment of paper. He is tall and a strongly-made man, but not stout; has a lurking walk, and as he walks, looks constantly over his shoulder, first on one side and then on the other; but I have only seen him twice, and both times he was covered up in a large cloak.

BROWNLOW. Upon his throat — so high that you can see a part below his neckerchief— has he a broad mark like a burn or scald?

NANCY. How's this? Do you know him?

BROWNLOW. I think I do; we shall see; many are singularly like each other, and it may not be the same. *(Aside.)* It must be he. What can I do to serve you?

NANCY. Nothing! for I am past all hope!

BROWNLOW. You put yourself beyond its pale; I do not say that it is in our power to offer you peace of heart and mind — for that must come as you seek it — but a quiet asylum at a distance, far from London; before the dawn of morning you shall be placed beyond the reach of your former associates, and leave as utter an absence of all trace behind you as if you were to disappear from the earth this moment. Come, I wouldn't have you go back to exchange one word with any old companion, or breathe the air of any haunt which is pestilence and death to you. Quit them all, while yet there is time and opportunity!

NANCY. No, sir, no; I am chained to my old life — I loathe and hate it now, but I cannot leave it! I have gone too far to turn back. But a fear conies over me again, and I must go home.

ROSE. Home?

NANCY. Home, lady! To such a home aa l have raised for myself. Let us part; I shall be watched or seen. Go, go; and if I have done you any service, all I ask, that you leave me and let me go my way alone.

BROWNLOW. We compromise her safety, perhaps, by staying her.

NANCY. Yes, yes! you do — you have.

ROSE. What— what can be the end of this poor creature's life?

NANCY. What! Look before you lady — look at that dark water! how many times do you read of such as I, who spring into the tide, and leave no living thing to care for or bewail them! It may be years hence, or it may be only months; but I shall come to that at last!

ROSE. Do not speak thus, I pray.

NANCY. It will never reach your ear, lady; and God forbid such horrors should! I must go back to him — good night! good night!

ROSE. Will you accept this purse?

NANCY. No! no! And yet I should like something you have worn. No, not a ring; — no baubles! no! your glove! your handkerchief! *(Takes handkerchief.)* This, this will for a last remembrance do. God bless you both! good night! good night!

ROSE. Good night.

(They separate and exit hastily.)

NOAH. *(Coming forward.)* Good night, indeed! Now, all this shall to the Jew! *(Exits right.)*

Scene II

The garret of Sikes.

Enter NANCY — Music.

NANCY. I think I have escaped unnoticed! Sikes has not yet come home; that's fortunate. I don't know how it is, but I have such a fear and dread upon me to-night that I can hardly stand; and I can think of nothing else but horrible thoughts of death and shrouds with blood upon them. I was reading a book before I went out to while away the time, and I'll swear that I saw coffin written in every page, in large black letters! Ay! and they carried one close to me in the street to-night; but I do not think it was real. I will try and sleep till he comes back, and his knock at the door will wake me up. *(Lying on bed.)* I dreamt last night that Fagin would bring me to an untimely end. How tired I am! I do not hate that man, but I fear him — oh! how I fear him!

(Sleeps. Enter SIKES.)

SKIES. The Jew has told me all — she has put laudanum in my drink — she has betrayed me. *(Rouses her.)* Get up!

NANCY. It is you? I am so glad!

SIKES. It is — get up! *(Extinguishes light.)*

NANCY. You've put out the light; but no matter, the day is beginning to dawn, and I'll open the window.

SIKES. Let it be! There's light enough for what I've got to do.

(Seizing her arm and dragging her to center.)

NANCY. Oh! tell me what I've done — I — I won't scream or cry; but speak to me and tell me what I've done.

SIKES. You know! You were watched to-night, and every word was heard!

NANCY. Then spare my life, for the love of heaven, as I spared yours! *(Clinging to him.)* You cannot have the heart to kill me! I will not lose my hold! You cannot throw me off! Oh, stop before you spill my blood! I have been true to you — upon my guilty soul!

SKIES. Off! Off!

NANCY. The good lady and gentleman told me of a home where I could end my days in solitude and peace. Let me see them again, and beg them on my knees to show the same mercy and goodness unto you, and let us never see each other more— let us lead better lives, and forget how we have lived, except in prayer! It is never too late to repent — never!

SKIES. You will not loose your hold.

NANCY. No — I will hold you till you kiss me and forgive.

SKIES. Perdition! *(Music. — He drags her off — A scream is heard, then a fall.— SIKES re-enters, pale and trembling.)* There is blood upon these hands and she is dead!

(Rushes out.)

SCENE III

Music. — SIKES enters. — Expresses horror at the deed he has committed, and dread of discovery, — looks cautiously behind him and steals off.

SCENE IV

A prison. Grated door, center.

FAGIN discovered seated on pallet.

FAGIN. One night more to live. A poor old man condemned to die. I didn't kill her, it was Bill. Ah, ha! They'll hang him, too. They'll squeeze his thick bull-dog neck. My God! twelve men to condemn a poor old man — a poor old man; my Lord! a poor old man. How cold and dark it is here. *(Beating his hands.)* I shall go mad. Good boy

Charley; well done, Oliver, too, ha! Ha! Oliver is quite a gentleman, now.

(Enter JAILOR, MR. BROWNLOW, and OLIVER.)

JAILOR. Here he is.

BROWNLOW. He seems quite crazed.

JAILOR. That's a pleasant state of mind for a man to die in, isn't it, sir?

BROWNLOW. Terrible, indeed; when is he to be executed?

JAILOR. In less than an hour; he's been raving like that all night, and he seems to get worse as the time comes on — they haven't caught Sikes yet — have they?

BROWNLOW. No; but they are in pursuit of him, and are sure of him before night. Speak to him.

JAILOR. Fagin.

FAGIN. Yes, my lord?

JAILOR. Now, sir, tell him what you want, now he's quiet.

BROWNLOW. You have some papers, which were placed in your hands for better security, by a man named Monks.

FAGIN. It's a lie, it's a lie! not one, not one.

BROWNLOW. Do not say that upon the very verge of the grave.

FAGIN. The grave.

BROWNLOW. Monks has confessed all, and they are in pursuit of Sikes.

FAGIN. What! haven't they got Bill; will they let him go, and hang.

BROWNLOW. You planned her death, and urged the villain on.

FAGIN. *(In despair.)* Oh, oh!

BROWNLOW. Sikes will soon be captured.

FAGIN Do you think so, eh?

BROWNLOW. But the papers.

(FAGIN beckons to OLIVER, who crosses to him, Mr. B. tries to restrain him.)

OLIVER. I'm not afraid.

FAGIN. The papers are in a little canvass bag, up the chimney in the top front room. I want to talk to you, Oliver.

OLIVER. Yes, yes — let me say a prayer — say only one on your knees, with me.

FAGIN. Yes, outside. Let's pray outside. Hush — tell 'em I'm asleep, they believe you; you can take me out so—

OLIVER. God forgive this wretched man.

FAGIN. That's right, quick — through the door; if I shake or tremble don't mind me, but hurry on.

JAILOR. Have you nothing else to ask him. -'

BROWNLOW. No. I would like to have recalled him to a sense of his real position. *(Going up.)*

FAGIN. Now, faster — faster, there is no one looking, faster— faster. *(Rushing up center, when the JAILOR disengages OLIVER from him, and all exeunt. FAGIN screams)* Ha! they've gone and left me alone to die. Here, Bill Sikes, Bates, Charley, where are you? Break down the walls and let me out! oh, if I had you here chained down.

(Bell tolls. JAILOR and TURNKEY with warrant enter. FAGIN, appalled ^ falls center—Tableau.)

SCENE V

Toby Crackitt's Garret,

Enter TOBY with candle and DODGER.

TOBY. And when was Fagin put upon his trial?

DODGER. Just at dinner-time.

TOBY. And so you made your lucky up the washus chimney, and Bolter got into the empty water-butt head downwards.

DODGER. Yes, but his legs was so precious long that they stuck out at the top, and they took him, too.

TOBY. I tell you what it is my fine feller, I wish that you had picked out some other crib, when the two old uns got too warm, and have not come here.

DODGER. I thought you would have been glad to see me.

TOBY. Why, look'ee young gentleman, when a man keeps himself so very exclusive as I have done, and by that means has a snug house over his head with nobody prying and smelling about it, it's rather a startling thing to have the honor of a visit from a young gentleman (however a respectable and pleasant person he may be to play cards with at convenience) circumstanced as you are. Well, well, it can't be helped now! And what's become of Charley Bates?

DODGER. He's lagged for life for a silver sneezer.

TOBY. Poor unfortunate individual. *(Knocking without.)* Who's there? *(Looking over the balcony.)* 'Tis he.

DODGER. He! Who?

TOBY. Why, he! Who could it be? And wretch as he is, I'll let him in, though I don't much like it. Yes, yes! He must come in. *(Taking light.)*

DODGER. Don't leave us in the dark.

TOBY. What, are you afraid? There, then, keep the candle.

(Music— TOBY goes to door and returns, followed by a man with the lower part of his face buried in his handkerchief, and another tied over his head under his hat. — He takes them off, and discovers his careworn and cadaverous countenance — -He staggers to chair and sinks upon it.)

SIKES. To-night's paper says that Fagin's taken — is it true or a lie?

TOBY. Quite true!

(A pause.)

SIKES. Confound you all ! Have you nothing to say to me? Do you mean to sell me, Crackit, or let me stop here till the hunt is over?

TOBY. You may stop here if you think it safe — I won't prevent you.

SIKES. Is it — the body! is it buried? *(They shake their heads.)* Why isn't it! What do they keep such ugly things as that above the ground for? What is that knocking?

TOBY. What knocking? All is silent.

SIKES. But the eyes! the eyes! Wherever I go they follow and look upon me! I can trace her shadow in the gloom — and how stiff and solemn it seems to stalk along! I could hear its garments rustling in Well, what are you all staring at? Toby, your hand. *(He turns away.)* Ah, Dodger, give me yours!

DODGER. No! let me go into some other room.

SIKES. What! Don't you — don't you know me?

DODGER. I do! — but don't come near me, murderer! Witness, you two, I'm not afraid of him. If they come here, I will give him up. Murder! Help! Down with him!

(Music. — They struggle. — SIKES overcomes him and draws knife.)

TOBY. Damme! don't kill the boy, or I'll kill —

(TOBY snatches up stool to hurl at the head of SIKES, when a loud clamor is heard without.)

VOICE. *(Without.)* In the king's name, open the door!

DODGER. Run straight to the room where the light is, or they'll never open. *(Seizing SIKES again.)* Let them in I say — break open the door!

SIKES. Open the door of some place where I can lock this screeching hell babe.

TOBY. There! there!

BROWNLOW. *(Without.)* A purse of twenty guineas to the man who takes him alive!

DODGER. Do you hear? do you hear?

SIKES. Silence! *(Thrusts DODGER into inner room and locks him in, then looks suddenly round him.)* Is the down-stairs door fast?

TOBY. Double locked and chained!

SIKES. And the panels — are they strong?

TOBY. Lined with sheet-iron!

SIKES. And the windows, too?

TOBY. Yes; and the windows too!

SIKES. Then damn you, do your worst — I'll cheat you yet!

(Rushes off right, followed by others.)

Scene Last

The roofs of houses. One very tall one center.

All the characters in piece discovered. — SIKES appears on roof. — At his appearance yells and groans are heard to welcome him. — He sets his foot against a stack of chimneys, fastens one end of the rope firmly round it, and in the other makes a strong running noose by the aid of his hand and teeth. — SIKES then shakes his fist at them in defiance; draws his knife and places it between his teeth.

SIKES. I can let myself down to within a few feet of the ground, and then cut the rope — stop! I will put it for a moment round my neck till I fasten it under my armpits. *(He puts loop over his head.)* Now Nancy! Ah, those eyes again! Hell! I have fallen!

(In turning his head he staggers and is precipitated from roof the rope tightens and he is left hanging, the mob below shouting "He has hanged himself" — Others overcome TOBY. *— Picture.)*

END

20081763R00034

Printed in Great Britain
by Amazon